REBOOTING YOUR YEAR

VE-ANNA
S.R. THOMAS

WESTBOW
P R E S S®
A DIVISION OF THOMAS NELSON
& ZONDERVAN

WestBow Press books may be ordered through booksellers or by contacting:

WestBow Press
A Division of Thomas Nelson & Zondervan
1663 Liberty Drive
Bloomington, IN 47403
www.westbowpress.com
844-714-3454

Because of the dynamic nature of the Internet, any web addresses or links contained in this book may have changed since publication and may no longer be valid. The views expressed in this work are solely those of the author and do not necessarily reflect the views of the publisher, and the publisher hereby disclaims any responsibility for them.

Any people depicted in stock imagery provided by Getty Images are models, and such images are being used for illustrative purposes only. Certain stock imagery © Getty Images.

Scripture quotations marked KJV are taken from the Holy Bible, King James Version.

Scripture quotations marked NIV are taken from the Holy Bible, New International Version®, NIV®. Copyright © 1973, 1978, 1984 by Biblica, Inc.™ Used by permission of Zondervan. All rights reserved worldwide.

Scripture quotations marked MSG or The Message are taken from The Message. Copyright 1993, 1994, 1995, 1996, 2000, 2001, 2002. Used by permission of NavPress Publishing Group.

ISBN: 979-8-3850-0201-6 (sc)
ISBN: 979-8-3850-0199-6 (e)

Library of Congress Control Number: 2023912336

Print information available on the last page.

WestBow Press rev. date: 09/13/2023

CONTENTS

ACKNOWLEDGEMENTS

I chose not to dedicate this book to any specific individual or organization. However, I am truly grateful to all the persons who worked behind the scenes and contributed in various ways to make publishing this book a reality. I thank you from the bottom of my heart.

This Book is Dedicated To
All the Rebooters
(PS. you will understand the term as you keep reading)

PRESS THAT BUTTON!!!

GET THE OLD OUT.
LET THE NEW IN.

FOREWORD

Pastor Ve-Anna Thomas – a woman after God's own heart. One who has transferred her purpose into a reality.

I have known this humble servant of God for over seven (7) years, and it all started at Second Chance Ministries, Church Sanctuary in East End, Tortola, where I had my first encounter.

I take privilege as I write this foreword as she moves to another level in writing a book that has come to light. As I reflect on the foreword of this book, it led me to "bloom where you are planted" that is the motto of the ministry that God has entrusted to his servant, Pastor Ve-Anna Thomas. Indeed, she has been a light in the darkness: a motivator, encourager, speaker, teacher, preacher, mentor, and friend. She is always ready and willing; and willing to serve.

Pastor Ve-Anna is a role model to many and very passionate for the things of God. Now, as the author of "Rebooting your year" book, she declares that is a time to remove the old wine skin and replace with new wine. A new approach of life and to be purpose driven, a time to reset – going forward. A time to plant and reap. Old things have passed away, all became new.

Let the blooming begin, it's time to reboot and take charge of the new beginning – bring forth it's time for "Rebooting your year".

Pastor Micah Lettsome

INTRODUCTION

I am reminded that if there was ever a time we need to rest in the arms of Jesus, it is now! If there was ever a time we need to come to the Lord, it is now! If there was ever a time, we need to draw closer to the Lord, it is now! If there was ever a time, we need the spirit of discernment, it is now!

WE CAN TRUST IN THE LORD
WE CAN FIND A RESTING PLACE IN HIM.
WE CAN CAST ALL OUR CARES ON HIM.

In May 2020, during a sermon I preached entitled "Rebooting Your Year", the Lord led me to examine something Paul wrote to the Church at Philippi. You see, Paul was a man on a mission, speaking about the excellency of knowing Christ. What a privilege!

Philippians 3:7-8 (KJV)

7 But what things were gain to me, those I counted loss for Christ.

8 Yea doubtless, and I count all things but loss for the excellency of the knowledge of Christ Jesus my Lord:

for whom I have suffered the loss of all things, and do
count them but dung, that I may win Christ,

Also, as I prepared for the sermon, the Lord led me to the same scripture in the New International Version (NIV).

Philippians 3:7-8 (NIV)

[7] But whatever were gains to me I now consider loss for the sake of Christ.

[8] What is more, I consider everything a loss because of the surpassing worth of knowing Christ Jesus my Lord, for whose sake I have lost all things. I consider them garbage, that I may gain Christ,

I agree with Bro. Paul and conclude that we all have lost some things. We have experienced hurts, disappointments, and setbacks in life. We have lost family members, we have lost friends and relationships. Let us go a bit deeper. We have lost hope, love, peace, and joy. In some cases, the lost list can go very long. During the loss, we can gain other things in Christ.

My friend, before I go any further, I would like to ask you a few questions:

1. Have you ever lost anything?
2. Did you gain Christ?
3. Or would you like to gain Christ amid the loss?

Let that soak in a bit.

DEFINING REBOOT

During the covid-19 global pandemic, in early May 2020, the Lord gave me the word REBOOT. Then, I kept hearing it in my spirit and so I put pen to paper.

I would like to begin this journey by defining the word reboot. Yes, this is a journey, and I am happy to invite you along with me. By the time we get to our destination, I promise you that you will say that the journey was worth it.

Somebody say, REBOOT.

Ok, you must excuse me because this book was initially a sermon and whenever I preach, I try my very best to engage the audience. As you go through this book, you will see this principle in effect.

After I preached the sermon at my local church in May 2020, the Lord gave me the instructions to turn it into a book. What you are holding in your hands and reading right now, is the result of my obedience to God and me stepping out by faith and putting my faith into action.

Now, I am very sure that we have all heard the word reboot before. It is not new. Sometimes we must reboot our phones, reboot our tablets, reboot our computers, reboot our laptops, reboot our internet boxes, and reboot other electronic devices.

And … sometimes, we just might have to reboot our lives and reboot our plans.

Somebody say the word again REBOOT. I need you to say it so that you can become familiar and remember the word. Praise God!

I found this definition online for the word reboot: it is a verb (/ ri:'bu:t/) (with reference to a computer system) boot or be booted again. For example, "the new value will not be in force until you reboot the system."

Hold on to that thought a bit and stick a pin on it because we are going to come back to it later.

In school, we learnt that verbs are action words. The word reboot is a verb, so it is an action word. In other words, it means we must get into action. From my limited knowledge, I do know that a reboot fazes out the old information and install new information or new updates. However, I wanted to get a better knowledge and understanding of the term reboot, so I proceeded to do some research online.

What is Reboot?

According to the research I did online, I found that reboot is the process of restarting a working device using hardware (e.g., a power button) instead of software. Also, I found that rebooting is sometimes necessary for the following reasons:

I. After installing a software program.
II. After installing operating systems updates.
III. To recover from an error.
IV. Re-initialize drivers or hardware devices.
V. And other reasons.

My research also revealed that to reboot the device, you must save and close all open files or apps before, otherwise it would be impossible to do the reboot. I found out that a computer's memory is a form of volatile storage, which means that it requires an uninterrupted supply of power to retain the data. So, when you reboot your device, any data held in the memory and not saved to the hard drive is lost.

What is the difference between a Reboot and a Restart?

Oh, I am glad you asked because there is a difference. Yes, during my research I found out there is a difference!

As verbs, the difference between reboot and restart is that reboot is (computing) to cause a device to execute its boot process, effectively resetting the device and causing the operating system to reload, especially after a system or power failure.

On the other hand, restart means to simply start again. The term restart refers to an operating system closing all programs before a soft reboot. We may restart our devices daily or every couple of days.

As we can see from the above definitions, sometimes it is necessary for a reboot to be done instead of a restart. There must be a rebooting process. I would like to pause and tell you that **the boot process is necessary**, to get rid of the old data, old information, errors and to let the new in.

In order to gain a better understanding of the term reboot, I continued to go a bit deeper in my research. I discovered that to perform a hard or cold reboot, you must press and hold down the power button on the device. After about 5-10 seconds, it should turn off.

Then, once the device is off, wait a few seconds and then turn it back on.

Remember, when you reboot a device, you need to ensure that open programs are closed. Then, the device should turn off briefly before turning back on. *Does this sound familiar?* I promise you that it not my intention to bore you with research and computerized terms. However, I promise you I am making sense of it all.

Take a moment and think about it. Breathe in. Breathe out.

During the covid-19 global pandemic, many programs, events, services, activities, you name it were forced to close or shut down for a brief period. Then, slowly but surely, a lot of these things resumed, and we heard terms like the "new normal". However, I believe, I strongly believe that the Lord was doing a reboot!

God was rebooting the churches.
God was rebooting the schools.
God was rebooting the government.
God was rebooting the sports industry.
God was rebooting the entertainment industry.
God was rebooting the workplace.
God was rebooting your business.
God was rebooting your family.
God was rebooting your life.
God was rebooting your year.
God was rebooting the decade.
God was rebooting your purpose.

God was doing a reboot!

Somebody say the word REBOOT. When I received that revelation amid the covid-19 global pandemic, I was speechless. I said "my God, my God ... REBOOT"

Essentially, a reboot "starts over" anything that might not have been working properly.

Also, during my research of the term reboot, I found that a reboot may be cold or hard, which means the power was shut off and turned back on.

Then, I discovered that a reboot can also we warm or soft, which means the system restarted without loss of power.

Finally, I learnt during the research that some may even refer to a reboot or a restart as the process of erasing the information of the devise and starting over.

Hold on to that thought because we will come back to it later. Are you still with me? I hope I did not bore you with all the research and information. I know it was a lot to take in. Somebody say REBOOT.

2

REBOOTING IS NECESSARY

I feel like so many things happened so quickly in just a short time. In 2020, I recalled many people saying *"this was supposed to be my year"* and *"2020 was supposed to be my year"*.

The year 2020 began like any other year. We were in anticipation of a new decade, the decade of the month (PEY). During this decade, we are encouraged to use our mouths and our voices. This can be done through a prayer, song, sermon, exhortation, prophetic declaration, reciting a scripture and other means.

As I reflect on 2020, personally I had a good but rough start. Looking back at the beginning of the year, I was sooooo excited! I was so full of anticipation for the new decade. For me, the year began with the usual week of services at my local church during the first week of January. Then, in mid-January, the BVI Christian Council organized one (1) week of Unity Services, referred to the National Crusade, where several churches came together and collaborated thereby showcasing unity in the Body of Christ.

The weeks and months rolled by and I was scheduled to travel to Texas, USA in mid-March 2020 for a graduation. My airline ticket was already purchased. I started to clear my schedule. Just when I was about to book my hotel, I realized things were shifting in the atmosphere. Covid-19 became a hot topic on the news, conversation circles, social media etc.

Within a few days' time, I saw so many changes and so many things happening. I saw businesses closed, events cancelled, people told to stay at home. I recalled the panic, the fear, the stress, and the anxiety began to creep in our lives. It all became so real.

Eventually, I cancelled my trip to Texas when I saw what was going on. I decided that I was not traveling internationally in the unlikely event that something goes wrong, I would like to be at home. Fear is real people. Also, there was the threat of the borders of the BVI closing. So many things were happening at that time!

Amidst all the chaos going on in the world, I was also dealing with some health challenges. I was dealing with about 4-5 different health issues at the same time. One day my body was not feeling right, and I went to the doctor just in time!

I had to change my daily routine. I had to change my eating habits. I had to implement meal planning and so on. I had to change my schedule and really stick to my planner. I had to cut back on some activities. I had to say NO to some things and rest. Yes, I had to ensure that I was getting lots of rest.

I had to take it very easy (and still do), be calm and avoid stressful situations. Looking back, I think that God was doing a reboot in my life. Most importantly, I had to make a conscious decision to take care of me. Self-care and mental health became priorities in my life. I had to fight for my life. I had to be still and to leave everything in God's hands.

Personally, I discovered that it is not everyone who knows or understand or can adjust to my new normal, but I must do what is best for me. I am thankful for all the persons who prayed and encouraged me as I faced that difficult season.

I have truly come this far by faith. I can truly say that if it was not for the Lord on my side, I do not know where I would have been!

Then, just when I was getting my head wrapped around with my health issues and everything else that was happening in my life … The covid-19 global pandemic happened. I remembered that I kept asking God, what are you doing?

But glory be to God I am still here! Now, I realize that it is all a part of the boot process, specifically speaking, MY boot process.

3

A LESSON ON REBOOTING

There were many individuals in the Bible who rebooted their lives, whether it was by will or by force.

I think about Naomi's perspective was that of a bitter countenance in Ruth chapter 1. However, by the time we get to Ruth chapter 4, she was a happy woman, and she was praising God.

I think about Jacob whose name was later changed to Israel. The trajectory of his life changed from that day forward.

I think about Abraham and Sarah who were childless, and God gave them a child in their old age. Also, God pronounced them as the mother and father of many nations.

Those are just a few examples, there were so many others!

There is one thing for sure, our lives will never be the same again once we do a reboot. I remembered in 2020, some persons were also saying that they cannot wait for things to go back to the way they were (pre-covid).

Truth is, things will never ever be the same again, ever. The covid-19 global pandemic has literally changed the way we do life. It has changed the way we interacted with each other. It has changed the way we travel. It has changed the way we attend events and other functions.

Would you agree with me that a reboot has happened? It was not planned but it was forced on us and we have to embrace it. Moving forward, we have to embrace the change and shift that has taken place. We must embrace the "new normal" and include it every area of our lives.

I know for a fact that so many people have struggled with this. I believe this has been the cause for the increase in mental illness and other social issues over the past few years, post covid. It is true that the rebooting caught us off guard. It was unexpected. It was painful. It was shocking.

We can learn and be encouraged from some of the Bible characters, that good things, positive things can come from a reboot. We need to look at the rebooting process through the eyes of faith and not fear. This was one of the popular slogans during covid "faith over fear".

My friend, your future is bright.

4

IT IS REBOOTING TIME!

As I mentioned earlier, the Lord gave me the word reboot in May 2020. I recalled that at the end of May, we celebrated Pentecost, which is a time of new beginnings and rebirth – it is a time to call out and bring forth the beauty of His glory and the unlimited potential God has seeded in all of us.

There are so many things hidden on the inside of us but sometimes it can be difficult to embrace after we have faced so many of life's trials. That is why the rebooting process is necessary. There comes a time when we need a rebirth or a new beginning. There comes a time when we need to reboot.

Let me just add this right here ... **THE CORONA VIRUS CANNOT STOP YOU!** As a matter of fact, no one or nothing can stop you!

It cannot stop your destiny.

It cannot stop your destiny your purpose.

It cannot stop your dreams.

It cannot stop your vision.

It cannot stop what God has in store for you.

It might slow you down.

It might cause some delay.

But is should not stop you.

And it cannot stop you.

In Jesus Mighty Name!

Praise God!

As I prepared my sermon, I was led to another passage of scripture, Psalm 138:8 (NIV).

The Lord will vindicate me;
your love, Lord, endures forever—
do not abandon the works of your hands.

Put a praise on it! Praise God!

NOW is the perfect time to tap into the grace and the favor of God. NOW is the time to break up the fallow ground in your life so new growth can come forth. I command you to press that button to get the old out and let the new in. Declare that this year will be rebooted or restarted in Jesus Mighty Name!

Also, remember that this is the decade of the mouth (2020-2029), so be careful what you say. I encourage you to speak life. I admonish you to speak positive things despite the negativity that is all around us.

Why?

Because your words matter, that's why.

It is not a mistake, error, or chance why you are holding this book in your hand right now. My friend, could it be rebooting time in your life?

Let me speak this into your life:

You can become ALL that you were created to be.
You will fulfill your purpose.
God has not forgotten you.
God is not done with you yet.

Go ahead and give God a shout of praise!

My friend, (ok I believe that we are sort of friends because you are still reading the book!) I know the last few days, few weeks, few months, few years were not easy. However, listen and hear the voice of the Lord that is saying, it is time to reboot! Try your very best to drown out the cloudiness and doubt from your mind. Believe it. Conceive it. Accept it. Do it. It is rebooting time!

Come on somebody! Somebody needs to press that button down and reboot.

Your best, <u>God's best</u> is yet to come!

You have unique gifts and a calling that this world needs. You have a personality that is unlike any other. Isn't it time that you start to impact the world around you? Isn't it time you start to fulfill your purpose?

Understand this, based on the principles of rebooting. The new updates cannot be installed into the system, your system unless or until you reboot.

I know the Lord has been speaking to you. Uh-huh, I know! In fact, some of the things have already been downloaded into your system and into your spirit (just like a device).

My friend, if you do not reboot, the updates cannot be fully installed. You need to reboot! I know the Lord has already downloaded into your spirit or into your system:

- A ministry idea.
- A new business idea.
- A product.
- A line of products.
- A new service.
- A business expansion idea.

- A pop-up shop.
- A course.
- A program.
- A movie.
- A show.
- A play.
- A fundraiser.
- An event.
- Family plans.
- Future plans.
- A book (PS. I kept hearing a cookbook in my spirit)
- A music release.
- An album.
- A song.
- A poem.
- A project.
- A recipe.
- Something strange (but do it anyway!)

God has been downloading …

So, what are the unique things that God has downloaded in you?

I encourage you to identify with what you are feeling on the inside. Maybe you need to write it down. Or maybe you need to speak with a good friend, a confidant, a trusted colleague or someone who will hold you accountable. Get ready to begin the rebooting process.

My friend,

I know you wrote it down.
I know you prayed over it.
I know you started to put plans in place.
I know you talked to some people.
But you also need to reboot.

You need to reboot the system so that it can take effect.

My friend, UNDERSTAND THIS, really understand this. The new updates have already been downloaded but unless you reboot like a device (phone, tablet, computer etc.), the new updates will not be fully installed and take effect.

This book you are reading is proof that rebooting works. This book was downloaded into my spirit. I rebooted my life, and I published this book BY FAITH in 2020. This book was initially released as an eBook however, many persons have been waiting for the hard copy. Through prayer, persistence, and perseverance, I pushed through, and I found a publisher to make it a reality. Rebooting works!

Also, understand that you have a choice to reboot NOW or to reboot LATER. Whatever option you choose, please make sure you reboot. God wants to do a reboot; will you join or allow Him?

God will reboot your job.
God will reboot your business.
God will reboot your finances.
God will reboot your health.
God will reboot your relationships.
God will reboot your vision.
God will reboot your mind.
God will reboot your year!
God will reboot your life.

I urge you to get in agreement with God and reboot with God. If God brings you to it, He will bring you through it.

Listen to this scripture from 2 Corinthians 5:17 (KJV):

> *Therefore if any man be in Christ, he is a new creature: old things are passed away; behold, all things are become new.*

Also, I love the NIV of the same scripture above:

> *Therefore, if anyone is in Christ, the new creation has come: The old has gone, the new is here!*

I want to tell somebody, THE NEW IS HERE! Somebody shout, THE NEW IS HERE!!!!!

Praise God, the old has gone and the new is here. This is what the rebooting process does. The old information or data gets out so that the new information or data gets in. It may not look so. It may not feel so but in the spirit realm it is so!

Go ahead and press that button, hold it down and reboot. The new things/updates are bout to take over your year! They are about to take over your life. New things, better things, greater things are on the horizon.

I went further and looked at the Message version of 2 Corinthians 5:17:

> *The old life is gone; a new life emerges! Look at it! All this comes from the God who settled the relationship between us and him, and then called us to settle our relationships with each other.*

Look at it! I dare you to look at the new! I dare you to stare at the new. I dare you to embrace the new.

When the reboot is done, you would be saying/singing/praising:

Upgraded to serve you better!
Rebooted to serve you better!
Upgraded for my purpose!
Rebooted for my destiny!

Again, I stress, **the reboot process is necessary.** Say it: "I must reboot, "I gotta reboot", "I will reboot my year", "I will reboot my life", in Jesus Name. somebody shout REBOOT!!!

No, you are not crazy, you are just a rebooter! Tell somebody, you are looking at the new and improved! It is the time to start again. Yes! Pick that thing up and start again.

You can handle the new.

As a matter of fact, you are more than capable of dealing with the new. Regardless of how you feel today or what life's circumstances look like, you have rebooted successfully.

Listen to this other definition that I found of reboot. I found out that reboot can also be noun, an act of booting a computer system again. For example, "be prepared for frequent reboots."

Sometimes, when some updates are being installed, the system must reboot and reboot and reboot. We need to remain patient and calm during this process. I know if has been frustrating, long and tiresome; but remember that **the reboot process is necessary**. Somebody says REBOOT!!!

There is a scripture that says, you cannot put new wine in old wineskins.

Mark 2:22 (NIV)

And no one pours new wine into old wineskins. Otherwise, the wine will burst the skins, and both the wine and the wineskins will be ruined. No, they pour new wine into new wineskins."

Get ready. Get ready. Get ready! Get ready to pour the new wine into new wineskins.

I know that the reboot process may seem hard, painful. I know that the labor process might seem long and difficult but push baby pusssshhhh!!!! Reboot! Do not miss this destiny moment. Do not miss this life changing opportunity. Fight! Push! Reboot!

Be determined to move forward with the vision. Remember nothing and no one can stop you.

HOW TO REBOOT

"My Reboot Plan"

How do your reboot?

I am glad you asked because I am going to tell you!

There are 5 points the Lord laid on my heart, that I would like to share with you.

Now that you are ready for action, please write your thoughts down in the space provided below.

I. Reboot starts with a vision.

What has the Lord downloaded in your spirit? This is not what your friend told you or a sibling or a spouse, but it is all about you. What would you like to accomplish?

_____

_____

_____

_____

_____

II. Get ready to change your thinking.

Rebooting starts in the mind. What are you thinking right now? What is happening now? What are the plans you are going to take to develop your vision? What are you hoping to achieve? What could be your first step? What would happen if you did nothing?

_____

_____

_____

_____

_____

_____

III. Learn rebooting basics.

Strive to become more Christlike by developing admirable traits, such as love, peace, forgiveness, and joy. The thing is, you already know half of what you need to do, so just do it!

List some areas where you can improve. What are your strengths? What are your weaknesses? What is required of you? List some rebooting steps below.

_____

_____

_____

_____

IV. Reboot with confidence.

What the enemy meant for evil. What the enemy meant to stop you or silence you, God is using it all for your good. Remember that nothing can stop you. What are your options? What opportunities lie before you? What risk(s) you can take? Write 3 things you need to do NOW to reboot with confidence.

_____

_____

_____

_____

V. Get ready for an adventure!

It is something new, so enjoy it. Have fun and embrace it!
Better! Bigger! Stronger! Wiser! Take notes as you go along.

_____

_____

_____

_____

_____

_____

_____

CLOSING

Somebody shout REBOOT!!!

In closing, let us go back to the foundation scripture from the Introduction of this book, taken from Philippians 3:7-8.

Philippians 3:7-8 (KJV)

⁷ But what things were gain to me, those I counted loss for Christ.

⁸ Yea doubtless, and I count all things but loss for the excellency of the knowledge of Christ Jesus my Lord: for whom I have suffered the loss of all things, and do count them but dung, that I may win Christ,

Philippians 3:7-8 (NIV)

⁷ But whatever were gains to me I now consider loss for the sake of Christ.

⁸ What is more, I consider everything a loss because of the surpassing worth of knowing Christ Jesus my Lord, for whose sake I have lost all things. I consider them garbage, that I may gain Christ,

You see, the author of this scripture, Paul discerned what was hindering him and preventing him from moving forward. He had to let go of all the things he once cherished, considering them distractions to grace. He even mentioned that he considered them garbage. In other words, Paul pressed the button to reboot his life. The purpose was to gain Christ and the things of Christ.

Will you?

What do you need to let go of?

What is distracting you?

What do you think is stopping you?

What is blocking you from moving forward?

What obstacles are getting in the way?

What roadblocks are you facing?

Are you stuck?

Are you willing to work through the impact that the past had on your life?

Are you blaming others for how your life turned out?

Are you ready to ask for forgiveness from others?

Do you think that you need the approval of someone?

Paul said, everything that was a gain to me, I considered to be a loss because of Christ. Then, he gets even more radical in verse 8, by counting his past accomplishments and even anything in the future as a loss compared to knowing Christ.

In Paul's opinion, he thinks that things are worthless when compared to Christ. The only way a person can view life from this perspective is to see and to know how valuable Christ truly is.

My friend, as you go through the reboot process, it is my prayer that you would see how valuable and how necessary Christ is in your life. Also, it is my prayer that you would recognize that you cannot reboot without Him. This is the gift or the present that is not wrapped in gift wrapping paper, but we must discern that it is a gift. I give you permission to open it and to use it. Go ahead take off the bow and the nice wrapping or arrangement and reboot your life.

I am recalling this inspiring message I received some time ago on some of the characters in the bible:

- Noah was a drunk.
- Abraham was too old.
- Miriam and Aaron gossiped.
- David committed adultery.
- Jonah ran from God.
- Paul persecuted Christians.

My friend, God chose them even though in our eyes they were disqualified BUT GOD qualified them. Child of God, you are still chosen even though through the eyes of some persons they have disqualified you and counts you out. God has a plan and a purpose for your life despite the hurdles, the trials, the obstacles, the setbacks, and the delays you have encountered in life.

My friend, do not let your past hold you back. My friend, do not let that one mistake stop you from moving forward or from rebooting. Do not let people's opinion hold you back. Shake off and close out the things that are holding you back to have a successful rebooting process.

Do you need to reboot?

Or will you reboot your life, your year, your month, your week, your day?

Right now, right where you are, look at your life. Think about how the year has been. Think about the last few months, weeks, days, hours, minutes. Think about whether you need to keep going as things are or whether you need to reboot. What are your hopes and dreams for the year ahead?

I love this song from Hillsong:

> *Though I walk through valleys low*
> *I'll fear no evil*
> *By the waters still my soul*
> *My heart will trust in you*

Yes Lord, I will trust in you with all my heart. I will trust in you with all my mind. I will trust in you with all my soul.

Lord, thank you for being our strength. You are our everything. We will trust in you with our whole heart, mind, and soul. Be with us as we reboot.
Amen.

My friend, thank you for joining me on this journey. However, the task is not done. Your work has just begun. Get ready to reboot. Get ready to embrace your new life.

I recalled one time I was flying from Puerto Rico back to Tortola, BVI where I live. As the airplane approached Tortola, I looked out the window and enjoyed the beautiful scenery. In that moment, the Lord gave me a word for when I returned to Tortola. The word was "POSSIBILITIES".

When I arrived at home, I wrote it on a piece of paper and stuck it on my bedroom mirror. When I got back to work, I wrote it on a piece of paper and put it above my desk where I can see it all through the day. I wrote it in my journal. I wrote it in my planner.

My friend, based on my experience with this word, I encourage you to see the new possibilities and embrace the new opportunities that lie ahead of you. You are a new creation. You are chosen and loved by God.

Isaiah 43:18-19 (KJV)

[18] Remember ye not the former things, neither consider the things of old.

[19] Behold, I will do a new thing; now it shall spring forth; shall ye not know it? I will even make a way in the wilderness, and rivers in the desert.

It is rebooting time! It is time that you live your life on purpose. It is time for you to be happy. It is time for you to be free and be your authentic self. I declare that you will no longer go through the motions because you have successfully rebooted. It is time for you to feel alive and experience contentment.

I give you permission to reboot.

I give you the keys to rebooting your life and rebooting your year.

MY REBOOTING PRAYER

Dear Lord,

I repent of all the things that are giving the spiritual forces a right to delay my progress. I repent on behalf of my life, family line, marriage, job ... Lord, anything that is stopping me, I repent. I pray for anything that is standing in my way and I say the blood of Jesus speaks for me. I declare that it shall be removed now in Jesus mighty name.

As a child of the Most-High God, I have the power over Satan. I crucify my flesh, my pride, and my ego. For I am a child of the King. I am royalty. Lord, I refuse to live in worry, fear, anxiety, and panic. Lord, I know that You are bigger than everything that is happening around us. I put my trust, faith, and confidence in You.

I know that where I am today is all a part of the plans you have for my life. I may not understand all the pieces to the puzzle, but I trust you and I trust the reboot process. Thank you for rebooting my life. Thank you for doing something new in me. Thank you for working all things out for my good, according to Romans 8:28.

Romans 8:28 (NIV)

And we know that in all things God works for the good of those who love him, who have been called according to his purpose.

Father, I pray that You will fill me with your power to live an abundant and victorious life. I receive the power of the Holy Spirit right now. Lord, today I pray for my finances. The economy is not my source, and my job are not my source. Lord, I thank you that you are my source and I trust in you.

Father, I pray that You will send the right people into my life. I decree that kingdom connections will happen this week, this month, this year. I declare that my destiny helpers will locate me. I decree Colossians 1:10 over my life today. I pray that I will walk worthy of the Lord, fully pleasing Him, being fruitful in every good work and increasing in the knowledge of God.

In Jesus name, Amen.

ABOUT VE-ANNA S.R. THOMAS

Ve-Anna Thomas is a multi-gifted servant of God who was born and raised in St. Vincent, a small island located in the Eastern Caribbean. However, she has resided in Tortola, B.V.I. for over fifteen (15) years. She is an Author, International Speaker, Pastor/Teacher, Worship Leader, Mentor, Administrator and Entrepreneur. Her life motto is "Bloom Where You Are Planted."

Ve-Anna has been saved for over two (2) decades and is a Godly role model for many persons around the globe. She has served in various ministries in the local church and at different levels. She has conducted the Lord's Supper (Communion), Water Baptism, Baby Dedication, House/Business Blessing and assisted with Ordination Ceremonies. Pastor Ve or Sister Ve as she is affectionately called, has sensed the need to become better equipped and enriched to serve God's people and she has completed studies in numerous areas, such as, Leadership, Theology, Christian Ministry, Evangelism, Counseling, Bookkeeping, Business Management, Paralegal, Effective Business Communication and more.

She is ordained as a Pastor under Cry of His Coming Evangelistic Association in Orlando, Florida, USA. Currently, she is a member of the Trinity Moravian Church in Tortola, and she serves on the Board of Elders, Vice President of the Women's Ministry, she serves in the Children & Youth Ministry and in the Christian Education Department.

In addition, Pastor Ve has accepted the mandate to advance God's kingdom by partnering with churches, ministries, and other organizations worldwide. Also, she serves on several executive boards locally and internationally.

In 2014, Pastor Ve answered the call of God to launch out on her own personal ministry, "Ve-Anna Thomas Ministries" that is now a registered non-profit organization in the B.V.I. She is transforming lives through her Holding on to Hope Devotion,

Bible Gleaners Online Bible Study, a "free" quarterly Leadership Workshop, and other initiatives. Also, she frequently creates tools and resources to equip and encourage individuals from all walks of life.

Pastor Ve is known for delivering simple "down-to-earth" but powerful impacting life-changing messages filled with empowerment, humor, rich knowledge, and in-depth research.

Pastor Ve has authored numerous bible studies, articles, blog posts, training material and self-published her first book in 2020 during the covid-19 global pandemic called "Rebooting Your Year". The book is scheduled to be re-released with hard copies in 2023 by WestBow Press, a division of Thomas Nelson and Zondervan.

Ve-Anna is single and in her quiet moments, she enjoys spending time with her family, reading, listening to music, and enjoying nature. She has endured numerous challenges, setbacks, and hardships for most of her life – but she believes that God is using it all for her good.

HOLDING ON TO HOPE
WEEKLY DEVOTION

AVAILABLE EVERY MONDAY MORNING

With Pastor Ve-Anna

FACEBOOK/YOUTUBE
@PASTOR.VE

BIBLE GLEANERS
ONLINE BIBLE STUDY

1ST & 3RD THURSDAY
8:00 PM EST C'bean

With Pastor Ve-Anna Thomas

FACEBOOK/YOUTUBE
@PASTOR.VE

DOWNLOAD FREE HANDOUT AT WWW.VE-ANNATHOMAS.COM

LEADERSHIP TRAINING PROGRAM

TAKE YOUR LEADERSHIP SKILLS TO THE NEXT LEVEL

WHEN: Quarterly
TIME: 8:00 PM EST Caribbean
PRICE: Free

Training is ideal for Pastors, Ministers Lay Leaders, Church Workers, School Leaders, Leaders in the Home, Community Leaders Business Owners/Managers/Supervisors & Other Interested Persons

LIMITED SPACES AVAILABLE
VISIT WWW.VE-ANNATHOMAS.COM FOR REGISTRATION INFO.
zoom EMAIL: VEANNATHOMASMINISTRIES@GMAIL.COM

FACILITATOR
Pastor Ve-Anna Thomas
& Special Guests

Leadership **ENCORE**

Leadership Workshops Available!

FOR INDIVIDUALS OR TEAMS
IN PERSON OR ZOOM

TAKE YOUR LEADERSHIP SKILLS TO THE NEXT LEVEL

Trainings are ideal for Pastors, Ministers, Lay Leaders, Church Workers, School Leaders, Leaders in the Home, Community Leaders, Business Managers/Supervisors & Other Interested Persons

SESSIONS CUSTOMIZED TO MEET YOUR NEEDS!
1-HR, 2-HRS, 1/2 DAY ETC.

FEE COVERS:
Live Training, Handout, PowerPoint, Certificate

SEND INQUIRIES TO: VEANNATHOMASMINISTRIES@GMAIL.COM

FACILITATOR
Pastor Ve-Anna Thomas

Here is a sample of daily encouragement you will receive when you subscribe:

A Prayer For Today

LORD, I DECREE AND DECLARE PEACE AND WHOLENESS IN MY FAMILY, COMMUNITY, NATION, AND AROUND THE WORLD. I PLEAD THE BLOOD OF JESUS AS OUR PROTECTION AND BANNER OVER US. AMEN.

DAILY PRAYERS | WWW.VE-ANNATHOMAS.COM

A Prayer For Today

LORD, MAKE ME AND MOLD ME INTO THE PERSON YOU WANT ME TO BE. LORD, I THANK YOU THAT YOU ARE OPENING THE RIGHT DOORS AND YOU ARE CLOSING THE WRONG ONES. AMEN.

DAILY PRAYERS | WWW.VE-ANNATHOMAS.COM

A Prayer For Today

LORD, I PRAY THAT YOU WILL
BRING LOVE, SALVATION,
DELIVERANCE, PEACE, JOY AND
HEALING IN MY FAMILY.
IN JESUS NAME, AMEN.

DAILY PRAYERS | WWW.VE-ANNATHOMAS.COM

A Prayer For Today

I DECREE EPHESIANS 1:4, JUST AS HE CHOSE US
IN HIM BEFORE THE FOUNDATION OF THE
WORLD, THAT WE SHOULD BE HOLY AND
WITHOUT BLAME BEFORE HIM IN LOVE.

I DECREE JEREMIAH 29:11, FOR I KNOW THE
THOUGHTS THAT I THINK TOWARD YOU, SAYS
THE LORD, THOUGHTS OF PEACE AND NOT OF
EVIL, TO GIVE YOU A FUTURE AND A HOPE.

THANK YOU LORD! AMEN.

DAILY PRAYERS | WWW.VE-ANNATHOMAS.COM

Has this message in this book encouraged you?

Share your testimony or feedback by contacting Ve-Anna Thomas Ministries.

For More Information:
Website: www.ve-annathomas.com
Instagram: @Pastor.Ve
Facebook: @Pastor.Ve
Twitter: @Pastor.VeVe
Pinterest: @pastorveanna
YouTube Channel: Pastor Ve-Anna Thomas
General Inquiries: Ve-AnnaThomasMinistries@gmail.com
Bookings: BookingPastorVe@gmail.com

Pastor Ve

ACCEPTING BOOKINGS
(In-Person & Virtual Events)

Available For:

CHURCH SERVICES
PRAYER MEETINGS
BIBLE STUDY
WOMEN CONFERENCES
LEADERSHIP CONFERENCES
WORKSHOPS
SEMINARS
OTHER MINISTRY EVENTS...
BUSINESS EVENTS
COMMUNITY EVENTS

Bloom Where You Are Planted

FOR BOOKING INQUIRIES
BOOKINGPASTORVE@GMAIL.COM
WWW.VE-ANNATHOMAS.COM/BOOKING

Also, you may use the hashtags #RebootingYourYear #ChooseToReboot

Printed in the United States
by Baker & Taylor Publisher Services